EVERYDAY STEM

HOW BLUETOOTH WORKS

AVERY ELIZABETH HURT

Cavendish
Square
New York

Published in 2019 by Cavendish Square Publishing, LLC
243 5th Avenue, Suite 136, New York, NY 10016

Library of Congress Cataloging-in-Publication Data

Names: Hurt, Avery Elizabeth, author.
Title: How bluetooth works / Avery Elizabeth Hurt.
Description: First edition. | New York : Cavendish Square, [2019] | Series: Everyday STEM | Includes bibliographical references and index. | Audience: 2-5. Identifiers: LCCN 2017048026 (print) | LCCN 2017056234 (ebook) | ISBN 9781502637390 (ebook) | ISBN 9781502637369 (library bound) | ISBN 9781502637376 (pbk.) | ISBN 9781502637383 (6 pack)
Subjects: LCSH: Bluetooth technology--Juvenile literature.
Classification: LCC TK5103.3 (ebook) | LCC TK5103.3 .Y87 2019 (print) | DDC 004.6/2--dc23
LC record available at https://lccn.loc.gov/2017048026

Editorial Director: David McNamara
Editor: Fletcher Doyle/Meghan Lamb
Copy Editor: Nathan Heidelberger
Associate Art Director: Amy Greenan
Designer: Alan Sliwinski
Production Coordinator: Karol Szymczuk
Photo Research: J8 Media

The photographs in this book are used by permission and through the courtesy of: Cover Praetorian Photo/E+/Getty Images; p. 4 Sodapix Sodapix/Getty Images; p. 6 Harald Wenzel/ImageBroker/Alamy Stock Photo; p. 7 Andrey_Popov/Shutterstock.com; p. 9 Pakula Piotr/Shutterstock.com; p. 10 Blend Images/Shutterstock.com; p. 11 Anetlanda/Shutterstock.com; p. 12 Courtesy Marjan de Ligny; p. 13 YanLev/Shutterstock.com; p. 14 Nednapa Sopasuntorn/Shutterstock.com; p. 16 Eric Audras/PhotoAlto/Alamy Stock Photo; p. 18 Julie Alissi/J8 Media; p. 20 Teerawat Chitprung/Shutterstock.com; p. 21 Dragos Iliescu/Shutterstock.com; p. 22 General Photographic Agency/Getty Images; p. 23 John Kobal Foundation/Hulton Archive/Getty Images; p. 24 Universal History Archive/UIG/Getty Images; p. 25 Saklakova/Shutterstock.com; p. 27 Monkey Business Images/Shutterstock.com.

Printed in the United States of America

CONTENTS

Bluetooth technology can help clean up this mess.

CHAPTER 1
WHAT IS BLUETOOTH?

Some rooms look like a spaghetti factory hit by a tornado. Wires and power cords are scattered over the floor. They connect lots of equipment and devices. They link computers to keyboards and printers. They connect game consoles to controllers. It's hard to keep all those wires from getting tangled.

Do your gadgets work fine without all the wires? If so, it is because of a technology named for King Bluetooth.

KING WHAT?

King Bluetooth had the gift of helping people communicate.

Harald Bluetooth was a medieval Viking king. He united Denmark and Norway. They had been at war. King Bluetooth got people to get along without fighting.

One thousand years later, some people from Sweden had

an idea. They wanted to connect **electronic** gadgets without using wires. Their idea was to use radio waves. Bluetooth was the perfect name for their invention. The Viking king helped people **communicate**. The technology helps electronic devices communicate.

Your remote control communicates with your television. The remote sends signals using

Your television remote control works fine—as long as no one gets between the remote and the television!

infrared light. Infrared light is invisible to humans. The light from the remote must go straight to the television. If someone steps in front of the television, the connection breaks. The TV won't turn on. You can't change the channel on the television from another room. The wall blocks the signal.

Bluetooth can't use infrared light to send signals. Devices need to stay connected even if something is between them. Also, Bluetooth

FAST FACT

Running Bluetooth uses very little power. Still, it can drain your cell phone battery. Lithium-ion batteries can be recharged quickly. They made cell phones possible.

Cell phones wouldn't be so useful without batteries that recharge quickly.

needs to connect several devices at once. You can't do that with a beam of light. Bluetooth sends signals using radio waves. Radio waves are **electromagnetic** energy. These waves move through the air. They are invisible. They can pass through walls. Each device or piece of

With Bluetooth, you can listen to music on headphones without any wires.

equipment transmits a radio signal. Each device or piece of equipment receives radio signals. This is how they communicate.

THE GOOD AND THE BAD

Bluetooth has many advantages. All Bluetooth gadgets are made to work together. It can carry voice and **data**. Bluetooth can connect up to eight devices. It's easy to install. Many devices come with Bluetooth installed already. Bluetooth solves the problem of too many wires.

Bluetooth has disadvantages too. Devices must be close together. Bluetooth signals indoors usually carry about 33 feet (10 meters). Bluetooth doesn't have enough power to send big files. You have to use Wi-Fi to send a big file. Also, Bluetooth drains power from a device. Plus, it's easy to hack into Bluetooth networks. You need passwords to protect your data.

Team Effort

Bluetooth was the product of a Swedish mobile phone company. The company was called

Jaap Haartsen is often considered the father of Bluetooth technology.

Ericsson. Its leader was Nils Rydbeck. In 1990, Rydbeck teamed with an inventor named Johan Ullman. They gathered a team of **engineers** to work on Bluetooth technology. A Dutch engineer named Jaap Haartsen did a lot of the work. He is considered the inventor of Bluetooth. Creating Bluetooth was a team effort.

FAST FACT

Radio stations transmit radio signals at a set **frequency**. When you listen to your radio, you set it to receive one frequency. Radio

With Bluetooth, multiple wireless devices, such as a keyboard and a mouse, can operate in one room.

stations close to each other aren't allowed to transmit at the same frequency. If they did, both signals would be heard at once. This is called **interference**.

Interference also occurs when several devices in one room are sending signals. Haartsen and

Radios hop from one frequency to the next as they search for signals.

his team solved this problem using frequency hopping. When you push the **scan** button on your radio, it seeks the next frequency. The radio will hop from frequency to frequency until you tell it to stop. In Bluetooth, the devices switch frequencies together. They switch very rapidly. This prevents interference. There is no radio wave spaghetti. The signals don't get tangled.

Devices with Bluetooth can talk to each other.

CHAPTER 2
HOW DOES IT WORK?

Bluetooth allows devices to talk back and forth. When you turn on a device with Bluetooth, it sends out signals. The signals are called an inquiry. Signals are special patterns of energy that other devices can recognize. The other devices scan for inquiries. When they get an inquiry, they respond. This connects both devices. Bluetooth devices need to be bonded to connect. A bond is formed by pairing. Pairing is like putting someone's phone number in your contacts list. A Bluetooth device will remember another device's contact information. Once two devices have been paired, they will always connect automatically. You don't have to do anything. A group of connected devices is called a personal area network. A network of devices connected with Bluetooth is called a piconet.

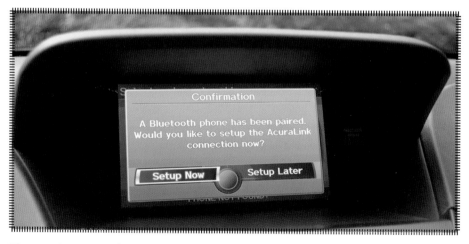

Bluetooth connections come in handy in cars.

In each piconet, there is one device that is called a master. It can connect to as many as seven slave devices. Slave devices can connect to only one master. The master sends signals to other devices. The other devices scan for those signals. The master also asks the other devices for data.

RADIO WAVES

Radio waves are invisible. Radio waves have peaks and valleys, just like ocean waves. The distance between the peaks is the wavelength. The number of times a wave repeats in a set period is its frequency. Each complete wave that passes is a cycle. You can count how many cycles pass by counting the peaks. Do twelve peaks pass each second? That means the wave

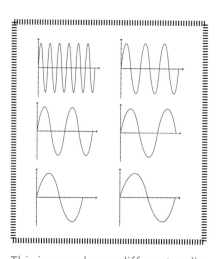

This image shows different radio waves. The closer two peaks of a wave are to each other, the shorter the wavelength and the higher the frequency.

has a frequency of twelve cycles per second. Cycles per second are also called hertz (Hz). A frequency of twelve cycles per second is called 12 Hz. They are called this in honor of Heinrich Hertz. He was a German scientist who lived in the 1800s. He proved that electromagnetic waves are real.

A few years later, people learned how to send messages using radio waves. They **encoded** messages in the waves. Guglielmo Marconi was an Italian inventor. In 1895, he sent the first message by radio signal.

CLEAN UP WITH BLUETOOTH

Bluetooth can help you brush your teeth better. An electric toothbrush with Bluetooth sends information to your cell  phone. It tracks how long you brush. It says where in your mouth you brush the most. It tells you if you're brushing too hard or not hard enough. It can let you know if your brushing is improving. You can share this with your dentist at your next check-up.

In 1901, Guglielmo Marconi received the first radio signal sent across the Atlantic Ocean. The signal traveled 2,100 miles (3,380 kilometers). It went from Cornwall in England to Newfoundland in Canada.

ACTRESS AND INVENTOR

Hedy Lamarr was an actress. She was called the most beautiful woman in the world. She was also very smart. She grew up in Austria. Her family was Jewish. She fled Europe before World War II. She signed a contract to act in Hollywood.

Lamarr wanted the Allies to win World War II. She designed a torpedo that was guided by radio signals. She invented an important technology. It was called frequency hopping. The radio signals would change frequencies as the torpedo headed for Nazi warships. This would stop the Nazis from jamming the signals. They would never know the right frequency to jam.

Lamarr gave her technology to the US Navy. The leaders in the navy didn't understand the technology. They didn't use it for twenty years. Now the military uses it for many things. It is also used in cell phones. Lamarr was given an award for her invention in 1997.

Hedy Lamarr helped make Bluetooth possible.

Frequency hopping could have helped guide torpedoes during World War II.

Today, there are many radio waves zipping through the air. They can get in the way of each other. Bluetooth doesn't use the same wave frequencies as radio and television. Radio and TV frequencies travel very far. Bluetooth's inventors found a better way to connect small devices. Bluetooth sends radio waves at very low power. Radio waves sent this way do not travel very far. They don't interfere with other waves.

Bluetooth uses the same frequencies as scientific and medical devices. Waves sent with very low power are also used in household devices and in Wi-Fi. You send them when you push a button to open a garage door. Baby monitors use them. So do cordless phones. Bluetooth's inventors didn't want their signals getting mixed up with other devices. Especially medical devices! Tangling those signals would be worse than tangling wires.

Bluetooth devices have to be very close to connect. This prevents some interference. However, interference was still a problem. It was especially bad in rooms with several piconets. Piconets could get mixed up with each other!

Bluetooth signals avoid tangling with signals for other devices, like baby monitors.

Bluetooth uses a band of frequencies around 2.4 gigahertz (GHz). "Giga" means one billion, so 2.4 gigahertz means 2.4 billion hertz. These frequencies make up one of the official industrial, scientific, and medical (ISM) radio bands.

Bluetooth's inventors found a way to keep this from happening. They improved on frequency hopping technology. Bluetooth signals hop from one frequency to another very quickly. A Bluetooth signal bumps into another signal? No problem! It just jumps to another frequency. Frequency hopping also keeps Bluetooth signals from fading. If one signal starts to fade, it starts fresh on another frequency. Data is sent over one frequency in small bits called packets. The devices hop frequencies in a set pattern. Another packet is then sent over another frequency. Bluetooth uses seventy-nine frequencies. Unconnected devices in a room rarely send at the same frequency.

Bluetooth uses new ideas and new spins on old ideas. That's how it solves the problem of too many wires.

A Bluetooth headset sends out packets of data to a phone, hopping from frequency to frequency, allowing you to communicate without wires.

TECHNOLOGY TIMELINE

1880   Wireless communication (radio) is invented.

1942   Hedy Lamarr files for a patent for frequency hopping technology.

1991   John Bannister Goodenough develops the lithium-ion battery, making portable electronics possible.

1994   Ericsson invents the first version of Bluetooth.

1998   A group of communications companies, the Bluetooth Special Interest Group, is formed to oversee Bluetooth standards.

GLOSSARY

communicate To talk or share information in some way.

data Information that has been changed into electrical signals.

electromagnetic Magnetism (attracting and repulsing) caused by electricity.

electronic A device that works by controlling electric currents.

encode To put something into a secret, or coded, form.

engineer A person who invents or builds machines or engines.

frequency The number of cycles per second of a radio signal.

infrared Light that has a wavelength beyond the range humans can see.

interference When one radio wave gets in the way of another radio wave.

scan Look quickly over a large area for a specific item.

FIND OUT MORE

BOOKS

Rand, Casey. *Communication*. The Science Behind. Chicago: Heinemann-Raintree, 2012.

Slingerland, Janet. *Wi-Fi*. How It Works. Burnsville, MN: Focus Readers, 2017.

WEBSITES

Exploratorium

https://www.exploratorium.edu

Science with Kids: Facts About Radio Waves

http://sciencewithkids.com/science-facts/
facts-about-radio-waves.html

INDEX

Page numbers in **boldface** are illustrations.

ABOUT THE AUTHOR

Avery Elizabeth Hurt writes about science and other subjects for children and young adults. She recently completed a book about climate change science and is working on one about code breaking. She would find it frustrating to work without the Bluetooth technology that operates her wireless mouse.